NATIONAL GEOGRAPHIC

T0288472

VIKING VOYAGES

PIONEER EDITION

By Fran Downey and Amy Ostenso

CONTENTS

VIKING VOYAGES

BY FRAN DOWNEY

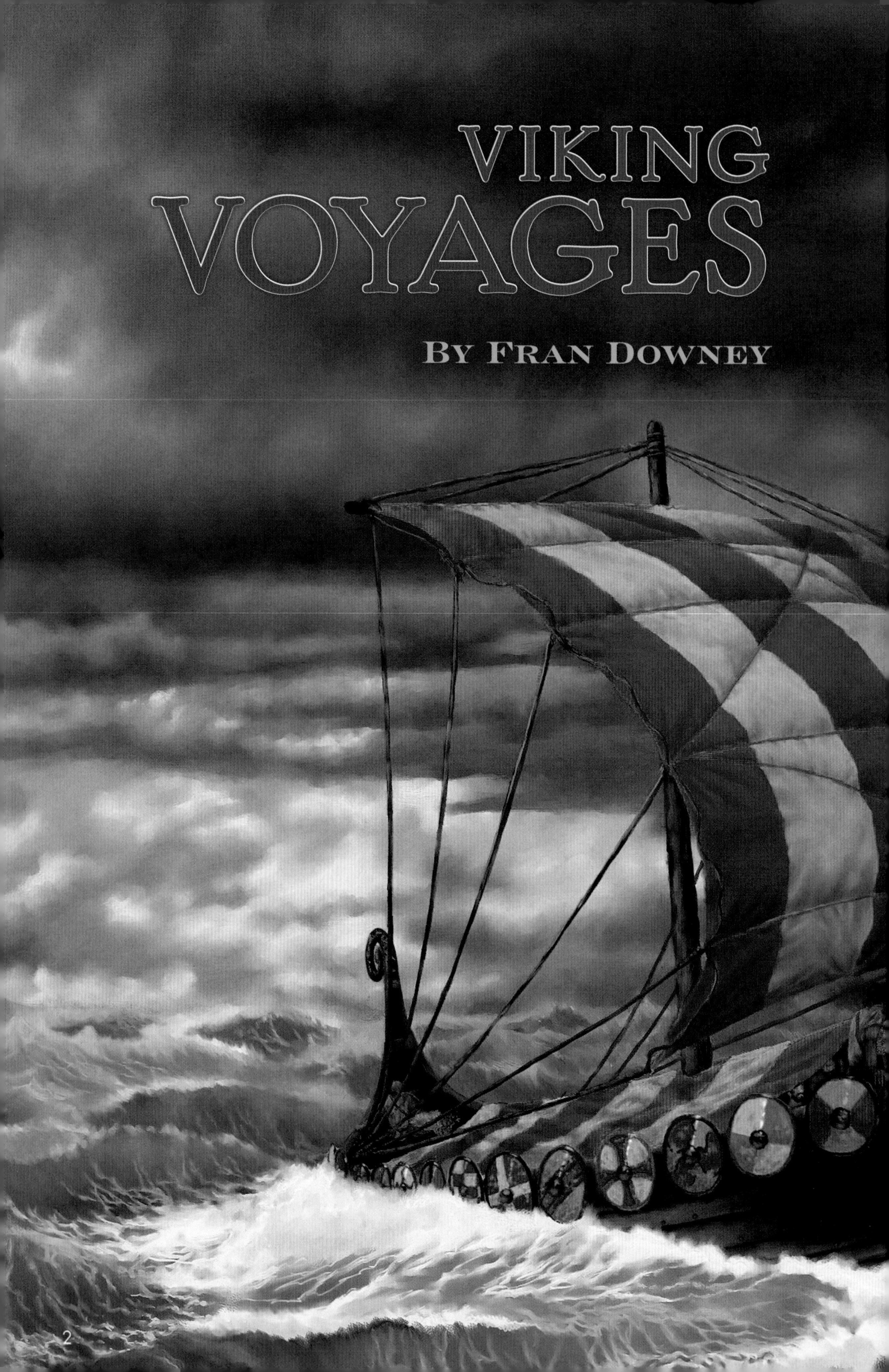

For nearly 300 years, the Vikings frightened people. The Vikings were fearless warriors. They stormed villages. They attacked fortresses. They stole gold and treasure. They captured slaves.

But not all Vikings were villains. Some were farmers and craftspeople. Others discovered new lands. They were the first Europeans to sail to North America. Yet their story is lost in the mists of the past. Now it's time to meet the real Vikings.

All stories have beginnings.

This one is no different. It begins on June 8, 793. That's when Viking ships sailed toward a small **island** off the coast of England.

The people of the island spotted the ships. The ships were still far away. It was impossible to see who was on them.

No one knew what was about to happen. No one knew that a new chapter in history was opening. They could only wait—and wonder.

Cool Cup. *This is an ox horn. Sometimes Vikings used horns like this as cups.*

Rowing Ashore

The ships came closer. Each carried a hundred men. Some of the men used long oars. The oars dipped into the water. As the men pulled on the oars, the boats moved forward.

Warriors sat with the oarsmen. Each fighter wore a heavy metal helmet. Some carried swords. Others held large axes. All were ready to take the island.

That's exactly what they did. As soon as the ships touched the shore, the warriors jumped out. They looted the island. They took everything of value. They loaded their ships with treasure. Then they sailed away and into history.

The attack on the island was the first Viking raid. It was the start of the Viking Age. For the next 300 years, Viking ships along the coast of Europe terrified people.

Village Life

Vikings are best known for their ships and sea adventures. Yet most never went to sea. Many lived in small **villages**. They lived on land that now lies in Denmark, Norway, and Sweden. Walls surrounded some villages. They kept enemies out. Inside the walls, people went about their daily lives.

Many worked as merchants and craftspeople. They bought and sold goods. Other Vikings brought these goods from faraway lands.

Villagers built houses. Builders stuck large posts into the ground. They put branches through the posts. Then they smeared mud over the branches. They used soil to make the roof.

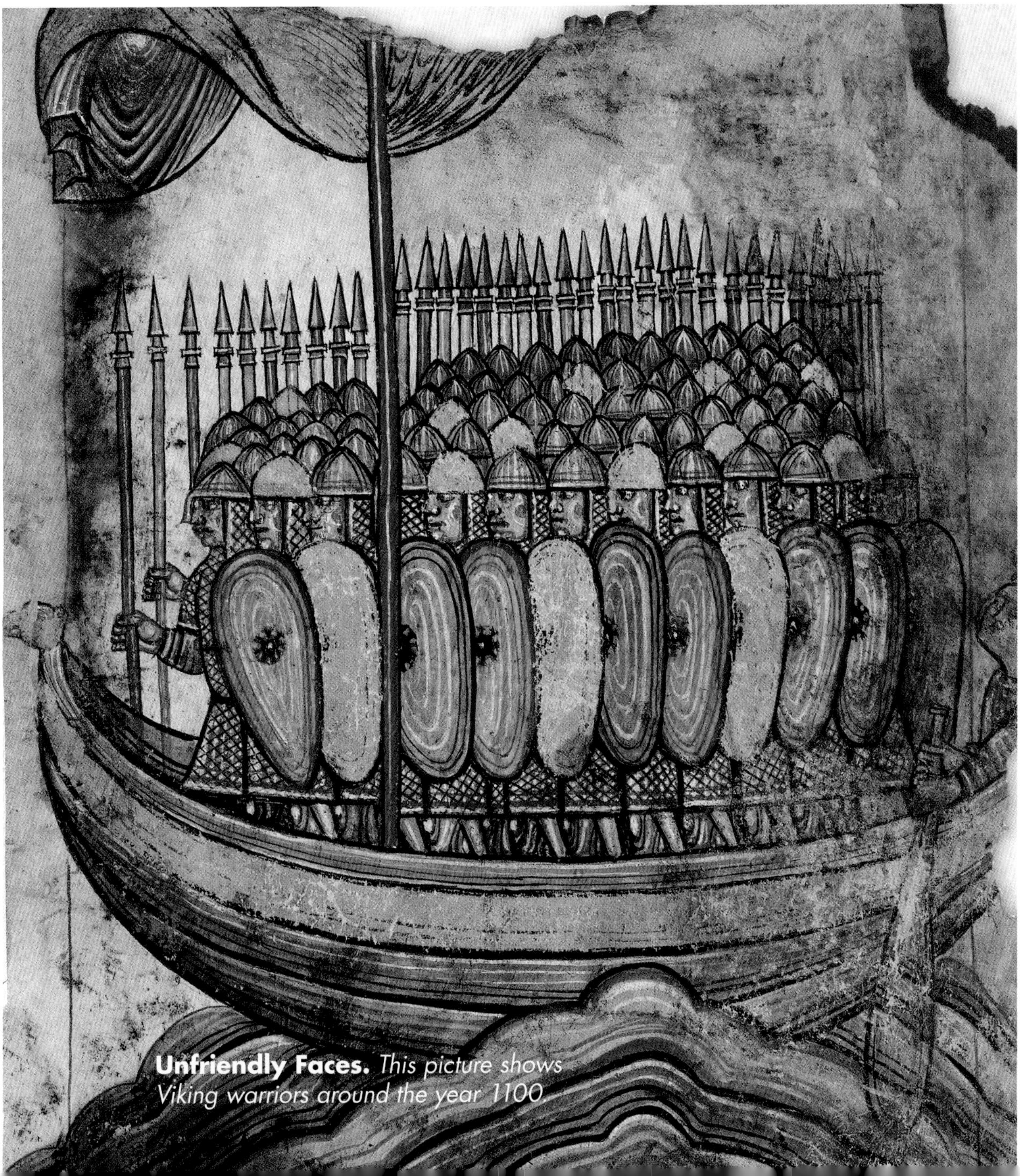

Unfriendly Faces. *This picture shows Viking warriors around the year 1100.*

Sod Houses. *Vikings may have lived in houses like these.*

On the Farm

Not everyone lived in villages. Most people lived on farms. They grew vegetables, such as peas and cabbage. They raised cattle. They ate beef and lamb. They drank milk from cows, sheep, and goats.

Viking life was busy. There was always work to do. The growing season was short, and winters were long. Farmers had to make sure they had enough food to last through the cold winters.

Still, Vikings tried to have some fun. They liked to ski and swim. They played chess and a game like checkers.

Vikings also practiced their religion. They believed in many gods. Odin was the king of their gods. He soared through the sky on a horse with eight legs.

Thor was another god. Vikings always knew when he was nearby. Lightning flashed and thunder boomed as Thor rode his chariot through the sky.

Some of the names for the days of the week come from these gods. For example, Thursday comes from a Viking word meaning Thor's day. Friday comes from Frigg's day. Frigg was Odin's wife.

Thunder God. *This statue shows Thor. He was the Viking god of thunder and lightning.*

Ship Ahoy!

Viking Coins. *Vikings loved their ships. In fact, they put pictures of them on their money!*

Viking villages were like many villages at the time. But their ships were different. Viking ships were wonders of their day. No one else had anything like them. The Vikings owed much of their success to their shipbuilders.

Each ship was built for speed. The hulls were designed to glide over waves. That made them faster than other ships. Large colorful sails caught the wind.

Some of the sails were 40 feet across. They pushed the ships over open water. When ships moved close to shore or up rivers, the Vikings took the sails down. They then used the oars. Ships had up to 50 oars.

These speedy ships were large. Some were more than 90 feet long. They could carry warriors and horses.

Viking Ship

Vikings used the sail to move across the open sea. Close to shore or on rivers, they rowed the ship with oars.

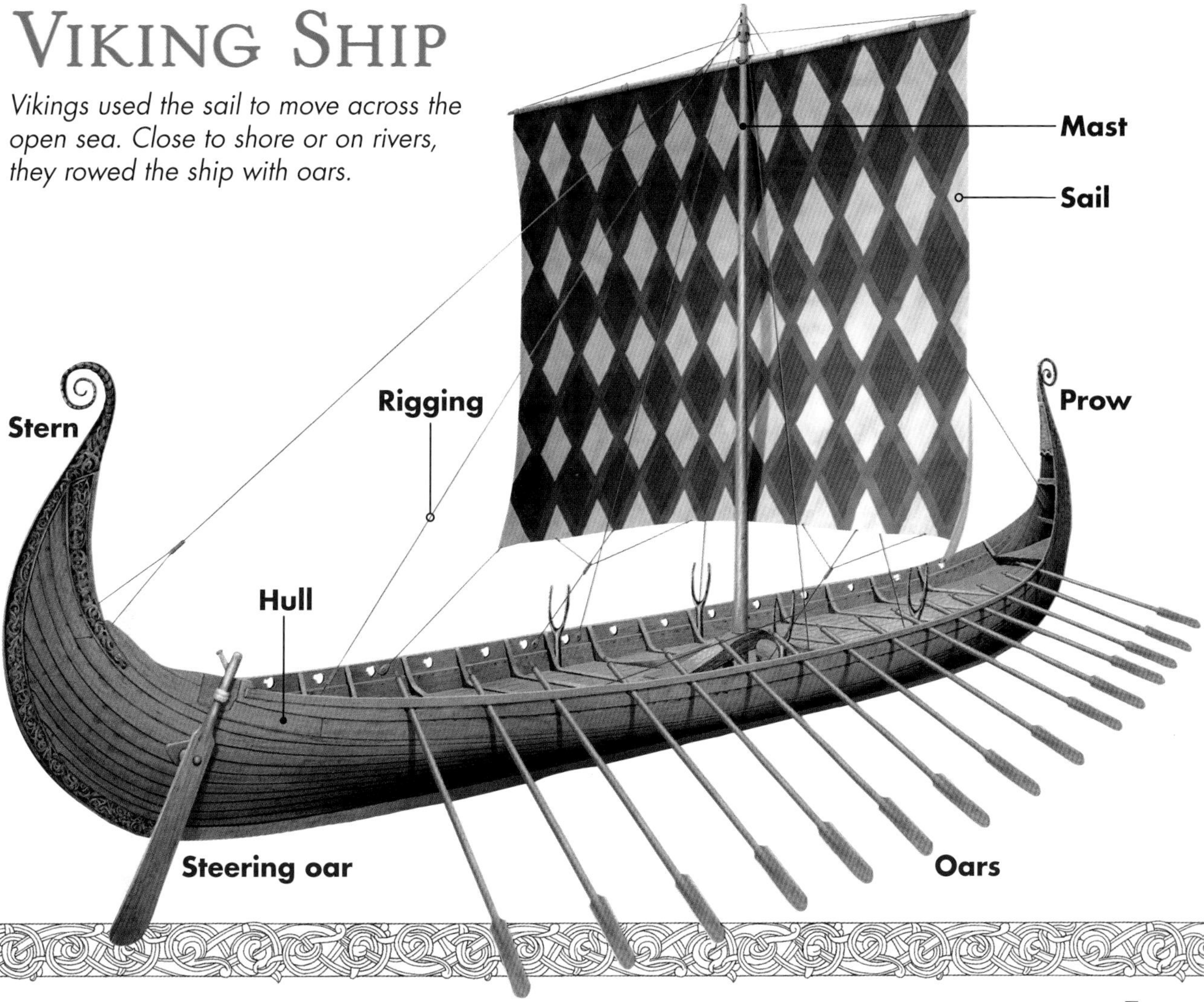

The Discoverers

Some Viking men left their families and homes to go on long **voyages**. They were often away for years. These amazing journeys took them to faraway lands.

Vikings sailed to England, France, Spain, and Italy. They went to Africa and Asia. They were the first Europeans to come to North America.

The trip to North America was slow. There were many stops along the way. In 860, Vikings reached Iceland. In 982, a Viking named Erik the Red found Greenland.

New Lands

These were exciting times. Vikings were discovering new lands. They were moving to new places. Then they learned about an uncharted land. Erik the Red wanted to go there. He never made it, though. On the way to his ship, Erik fell off his horse. Fearing bad luck, he canceled the trip.

Erik's son, Leif Eriksson, made the voyage later. About 1000, he found a new land. He named the new land Vinland. It was the East Coast of North America. He probably sailed along the coast. He may have even sailed to what is now New York City.

Vinland Voyagers. *The picture below shows Vikings arriving at Vinland around the year 1000.*

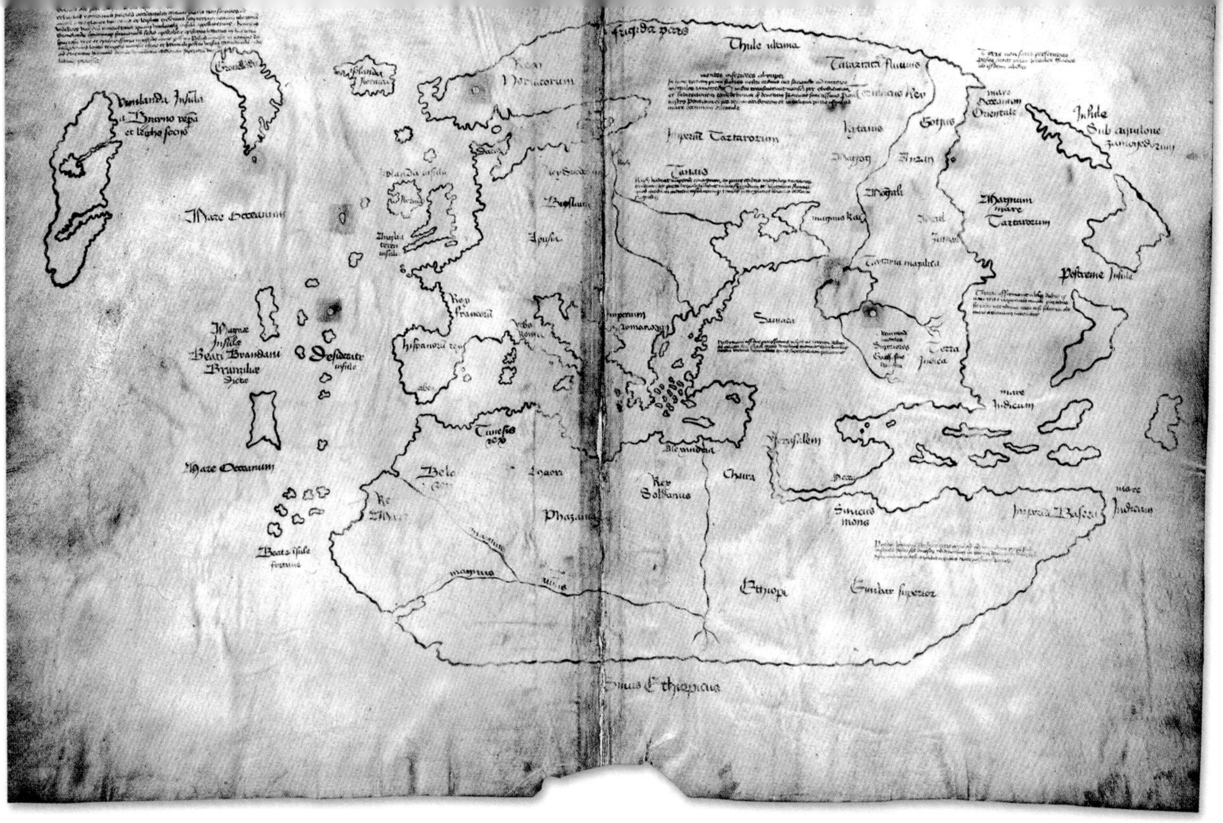

Vinland Map

Mystery Map

There is much evidence that Vikings settled in North America. Old legends tell of their Vinland adventures. Archaeologists have found a Viking village in Canada. There may even be a Viking map that shows Vinland.

The map is a bit faded. You can see parts of Europe clearly drawn. You can also see Iceland and Greenland. Beyond those islands is Vinland. It doesn't look much like North America. After all, Vikings only knew about a small part of the **continent**.

Not everyone agrees that Vikings drew this map. Some think it's a fake. It's the only map showing Viking discoveries. Why make just one map? No one knows.

The map is just one more mystery about the Vikings. Scientists are still searching for more clues about the Vikings' past. Perhaps we will never know their full story. Yet one thing is sure. The Vikings' colorful stories are an important part of history.

WORDWISE

continent: large landmass

island: land that is completely surrounded by water

village: a small town

voyage: a long trip on a ship

VOYAGES OF DISCOVERY

By Amy Ostenso

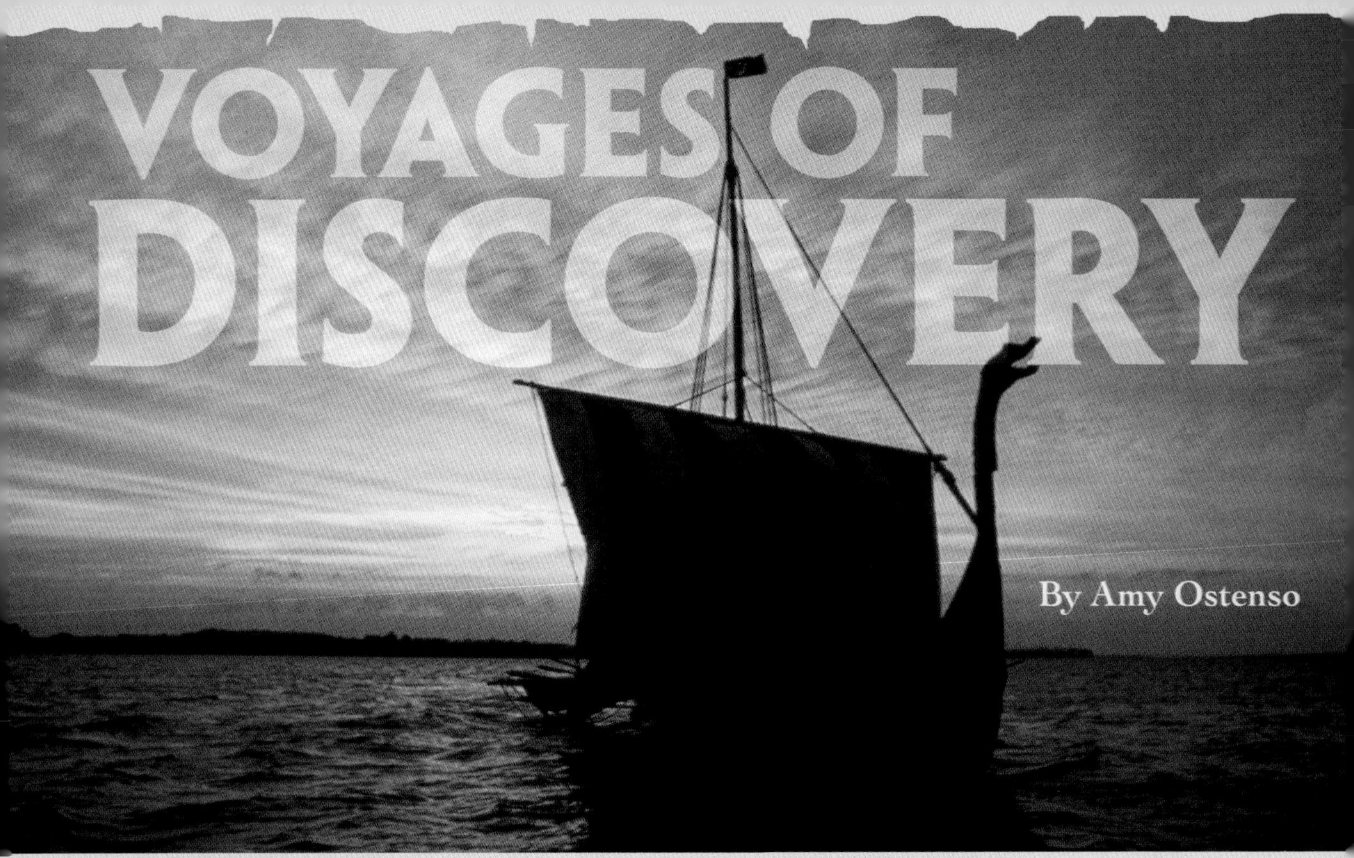

Viking warriors sailed south. They raided settlements. They took gold and treasure.

Erik the Red and Leif Eriksson were different. These Vikings were explorers. They knew stories about strange lands in the west. They wanted to find these lands and see if the stories were true.

At that time, it was dangerous to sail across the ocean. There were no accurate maps or modern tools.

Most ships sailed in sight of land. Sailors looked for familiar sights, or landmarks. So they did not get lost.

Vikings explorers sailed far from land for many days. How did they know where to go? Here's how!

PATTERNS OF CLOUDS

Clouds usually form over land. When sailors saw clouds in the distance, they knew land was nearby.

NEW TOOLS

Some scientists think the Vikings invented a tool. It showed sailors how far north or south they were.

The tool is called a sun compass. Only two have been found. Others think they were not used for this.

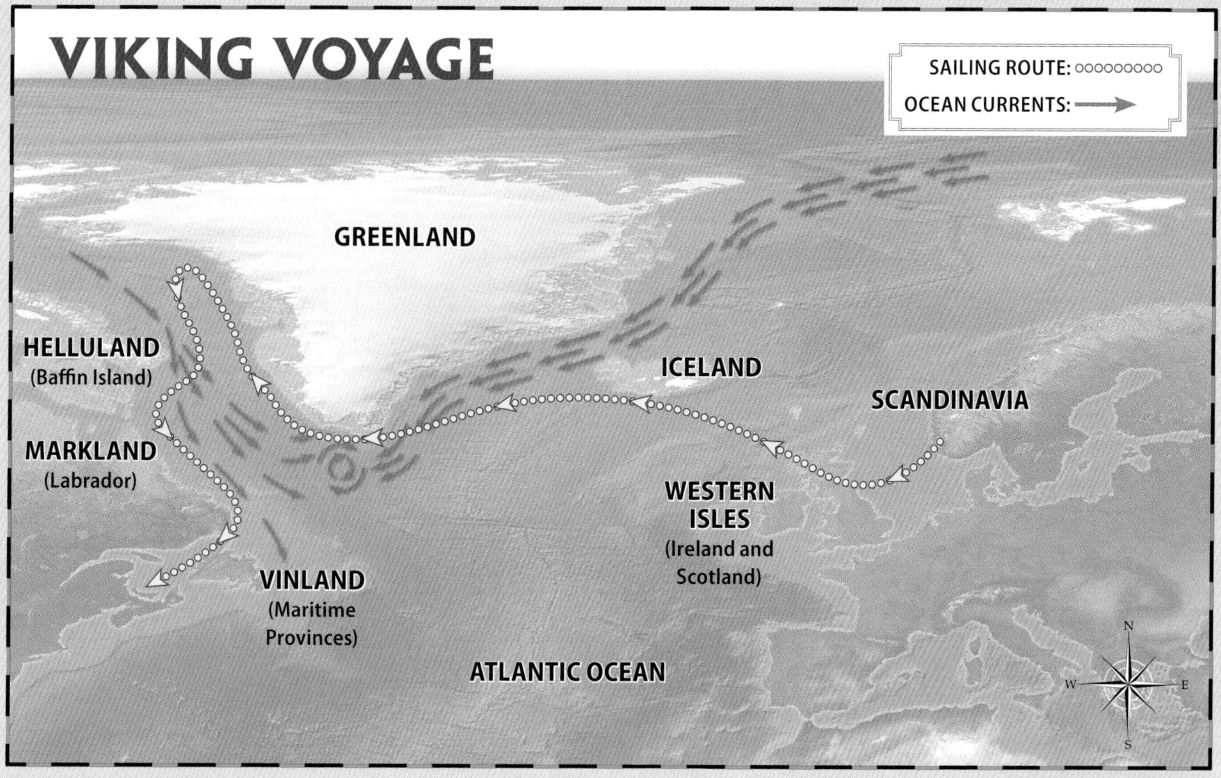

WINDS AND CURRENTS

Some winds and currents are steady. They move in the same direction all the time. Vikings sailors followed the winds and currents across the ocean.

SUN AND STARS

Sailors used the sun and stars to find directions. As it travels, the sun moves from east to west. The star Polaris points north.

Viking sun compass

FLIGHT OF BIRDS

Many birds spend a lot of time over the ocean. But they breed on land. So sailors looked for these birds. Then they followed the birds to find land.

Atlantic Puffin

It was terrifying and dangerous to sail across the ocean. But Viking explorers wanted to take the risk. They hoped to find new lands. They hoped their discoveries would make them rich and famous. And they simply wanted to see what was out there.

Viking Quest

Answer these questions. Then begin your own voyage of discovery.

1. Why were people afraid of the Vikings?
2. How did the Vikings live when they were at home?
3. What was special about Viking ships?
4. Name two methods Vikings used to find their way across the ocean.
5. How did Viking explorers make history?

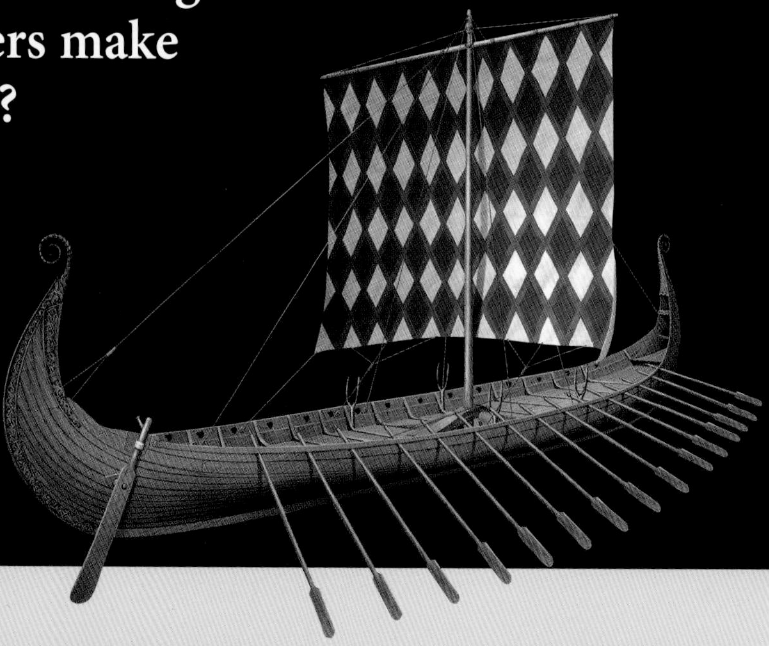